'Ere We Go!

David Orme lives in Winchester and supports Stoke City. He has written a wide variety of poetry text books and picture books for young children. He spends a great deal of his time in schools performing and writing poetry, and encouraging children and teachers to take an active interest in poetry.

Ian Blackman was born in Hastings and supports Brighton and Hove Albion. An ex-PE teacher, he now lives in Norfolk and runs workshops, using sport as a natural inspiration to write. His ambition is to be writer-in-residence for a football club . . .

Marc Vyvyan-Jones lives in Bristol and supports Bristol City (the Robins).

'ERE WE CO !

Football poems

chosen by David Orme

With football facts

by Ian Blackman

Illustrated by Marc Vyvyan-Jones

MACMILLAN
CHILDREN'S BOOKS

First published 1993 by Pan Macmillan Children's Books
This edition reprinted 1995 by Macmillan Children's Books
a division of Macmillan Publishers Limited
25 Eccleston Place London SW1W 9NF
Basingstoke and Oxford
www.macmillan.co.uk

Associated companies throughout the world

ISBN 0 330 32986 3

19 18 17 16 15 14

A CIP catalogue record for this book is available
from the British Library.

Phototypeset by Intype, London
Printed and bound in Great Britain by
Mackays of Chatham PLC, Chatham, Kent

Contents

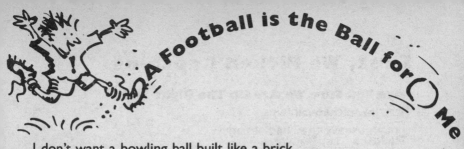

A Football is the Ball for Me

I don't want a bowling ball built like a brick
and volleyball is horri-ball, it gets on my wick.
I want a ball, a ball, a ball you can kick.

I wouldn't want to hit it with a wooden hockey stick
and to chuck it at a wicket in cricket is sick.
I want a ball, a ball, a ball you can kick.

My superball'll bounce off a wall dead quick
but a ball so small ain't at all worth a flick.
I want a ball, a ball, a ball you can kick.

Though netball's cool and baseball's slick,
there's only one ball game they just can't lick.
I want a ball, a ball, a ball you can kick.

One ball I need. One ball I'd pick.
I don't want six for a juggling trick.
I want a ball, a ball, a ball you can kick.

There's just one game with which I click.
Football, through thin and thick.
Football wins my voting tick.
Football, or my name's not Nick.

> So I want a ball
> a real ball
> a proper ball
> a ball you can kick.

Nick Toczek
Bradford

First, We Picked Captains

First, we picked captains,
though usually they had already
picked themselves.
Sometimes they just said it,
'I'll be captain,' and we pretended
our happy agreement.
It was easier that way,
and dusk was falling
so we needed to get started.

We stood in a line and the captains picked us.
'My first pick,' one would usually say,
and the other agreed, because that was easier,
and he never wanted
the boy that Billy picked anyway.

After they picked us, we lined up behind them,
always knowing who should be last.
But sometimes it happened
the usual last hadn't come to play,
had the bellyache, or was looking after
his little sister,
and someone else stood not wanting to be
the one not chosen, the one left over –
who never even got in the line with the captain
because already the rest were piling
their goalpost jackets and spreading for 'centre'.

Then, even the last-chosen would chase like mad
for a miracle goal, and their wild admiration –
though soon the ball was getting greasy
in the dew-sodden grass, and skidded away
off your boot in the wrong direction,
and the other side took it and easily scored,
and everyone shouted you'd kicked the wrong way.

John Loveday
   Norwich

The Ball Talks in its Changing Room

I'm the star really. I'm the one
the crowds have come to watch.
I don't let it worry me. Before the match
they check me carefully, make sure
I'm really fit. After all
I have to take more pressure
than the rest of them. And then
it's the usual jokes about
there being more hot air in
the commentators than in me,
and the ref puts his arm around
my shoulders and says he hopes
I'll have a good game, no need
for a substitute, and off we go
to lead the players out. No time
for second thoughts once we start:
I'm in the middle of it all the way
with everybody shouting for me,
cheering as I dodge around the tackles,
or slide out of reach of players
who just want to put the boot in.
The crowd is all for me, willing me on,
praying that I'll reach the net,
and when I do, roaring with delight.
I take it as my due. The lads are all right
but, when all's said and done, Desmond,
they'd be nothing without me.

Dave Calder
Dundee United

I'm Jennifer Jones

(or Antelope Jones...)

I'm Jennifer Jones and I make 'em all gasp
as I steal the ball neatly out of their grasp
pass to the centre and dodge to the side
skipping away from a tackling slide
collecting the cross that follows the throw
and shoot for the goal like a shaft from a bow.

I'm Jennifer Jones and I play on the wing;
I turn on a penny and I make the ball sing
as it curves and it spins past the gloves
on the hands of the keeper who LOVES
landing in mud and picking the ball
from the back of the net where I place 'em all!

Trevor Millum
Hamilton Academicals

Playing for the School

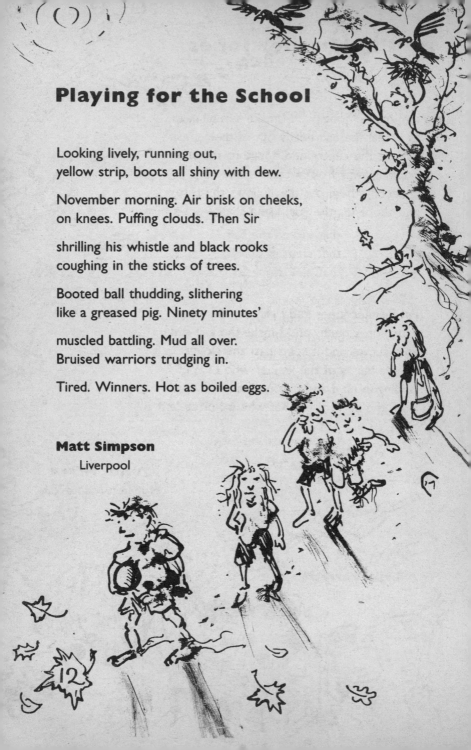

Looking lively, running out,
yellow strip, boots all shiny with dew.

November morning. Air brisk on cheeks,
on knees. Puffing clouds. Then Sir

shrilling his whistle and black rooks
coughing in the sticks of trees.

Booted ball thudding, slithering
like a greased pig. Ninety minutes'

muscled battling. Mud all over.
Bruised warriors trudging in.

Tired. Winners. Hot as boiled eggs.

Matt Simpson
   Liverpool

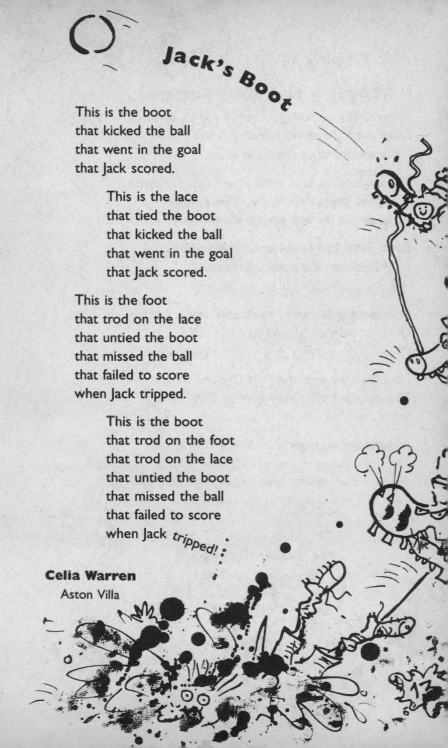

Jack's Boot

This is the boot
that kicked the ball
that went in the goal
that Jack scored.

This is the lace
that tied the boot
that kicked the ball
that went in the goal
that Jack scored.

This is the foot
that trod on the lace
that untied the boot
that missed the ball
that failed to score
when Jack tripped.

This is the boot
that trod on the foot
that trod on the lace
that untied the boot
that missed the ball
that failed to score
when Jack *tripped!*

Celia Warren
Aston Villa

My Glory

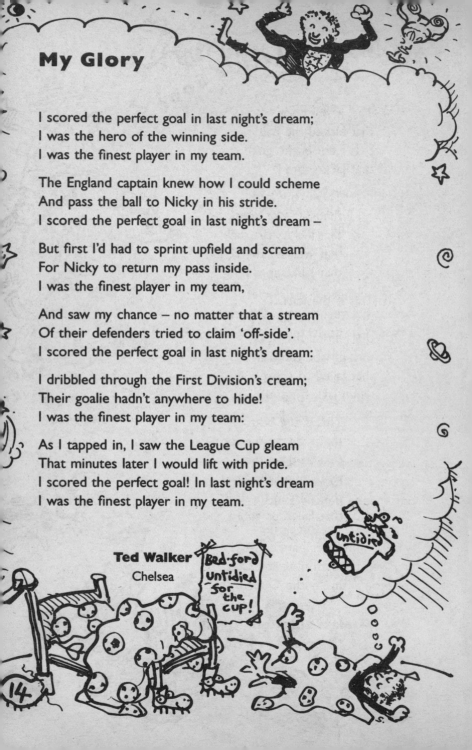

I scored the perfect goal in last night's dream;
I was the hero of the winning side.
I was the finest player in my team.

The England captain knew how I could scheme
And pass the ball to Nicky in his stride.
I scored the perfect goal in last night's dream —

But first I'd had to sprint upfield and scream
For Nicky to return my pass inside.
I was the finest player in my team,

And saw my chance — no matter that a stream
Of their defenders tried to claim 'off-side'.
I scored the perfect goal in last night's dream:

I dribbled through the First Division's cream;
Their goalie hadn't anywhere to hide!
I was the finest player in my team:

As I tapped in, I saw the League Cup gleam
That minutes later I would lift with pride.
I scored the perfect goal! In last night's dream
I was the finest player in my team.

Ted Walker
Chelsea

14

Football Mad

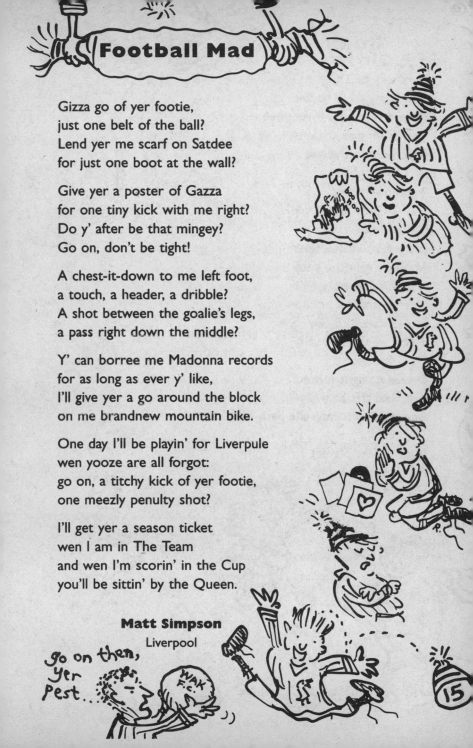

Gizza go of yer footie,
just one belt of the ball?
Lend yer me scarf on Satdee
for just one boot at the wall?

Give yer a poster of Gazza
for one tiny kick with me right?
Do y' after be that mingey?
Go on, don't be tight!

A chest-it-down to me left foot,
a touch, a header, a dribble?
A shot between the goalie's legs,
a pass right down the middle?

Y' can borree me Madonna records
for as long as ever y' like,
I'll give yer a go around the block
on me brandnew mountain bike.

One day I'll be playin' for Liverpule
wen yooze are all forgot:
go on, a titchy kick of yer footie,
one meezly penulty shot?

I'll get yer a season ticket
wen I am in The Team
and wen I'm scorin' in the Cup
you'll be sittin' by the Queen.

Matt Simpson
Liverpool

go on then,
yer
Pest...

Goal!

It's Dicky to Dirty,
And Dirty back to Dicky ...
He swerves past three men
    (Oh, he's tricky)
And he lofts the ball
Into the middle,
A pin-point pass,
    Which finds Diddle;
Diddle back-heels
(Very neat, that, clever!)
And lays it in the path
    Of Trevor,
Our six million pound
Striker (well 25 pee
If you want the truth)
    And he
Drives it, right-footed;
It strikes the bar
And rebounds into the path
    Of Pa
(Our oldest player)
But unluckily it hits
His walking stick ...

He sits
Suddenly, and the ball
Trickles back to Trevor,
Who shoots! ! Unstoppable! ! !
    Did you ever! ? ! ?
Their goalie palms
It away but straight
To Dozy (who's asleep) . . .
    But wait . . . !
Patch has got the ball
(He's half collie –
Recently signed from Rovers)
    And, golly!
He's nose down, tail up –
He's running rings
Round a sheepish defence –
    He brings
The leather to the educated feet
Of Gerard* (You bet!)
Now one neat flick and it's
    In the Net!

Gerard Benson
    Arsenal

* Or, if you wish,
put in your own name
as a late substitute . . .

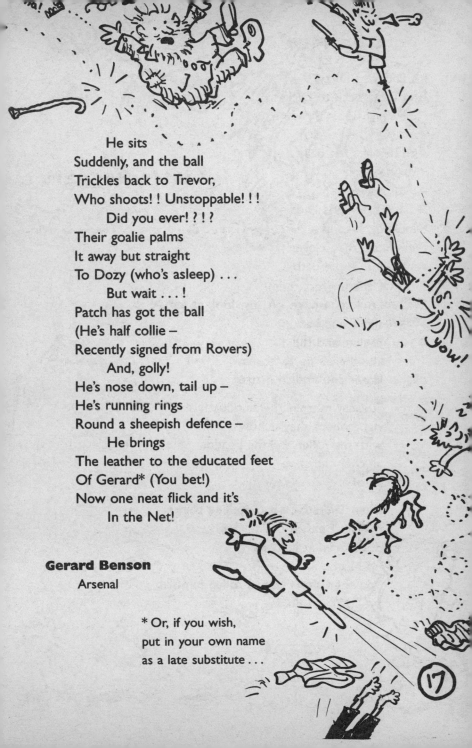

Little Beggars

Little beggers them!
Look at 'em, go on, just look at 'em —
slidin' and hackin'
hackin' and slidin'
like there's no tomorrow,
like it don't much matter.

Tuesday mornin', I was out there
right where they is now
with me roller and me prodder
all over the shop
all of it.

Then Thursday, I had me line painter
that ain't easy, I can tell yer
not like what it looks —
no Mister.
You soon see if you've rolled him flat
aye, that yer do.

Then this mornin', I was here at five
before all those horrible rough boys
was up, I'll be bound,
puttin' in them flags
and hangin' nets
and unlocking changin' rooms.

Not that you'd credit it
lookin' at it now
it's a proper disgrace
– shouldn't be allowed.

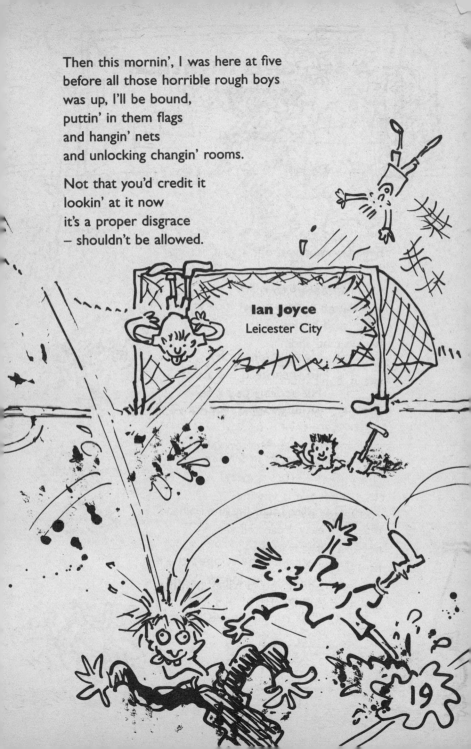

Ian Joyce
Leicester City

19

A Striker's Nightmare

Twelve games without a goal,
His leanest time in years.
His head begins to roll
Tormented by the jeers.

He cost a hefty fee
To spearhead the attack.
His scoring pedigree
Now stretches on the rack.

He scores the goals in training
And puts the crosses away.
His confidence is waning
'You've got to score today.'

Last week he scraped the bar,
And also hit a post.
He wears it like a scar
This run he dreads the most.

The winger tricks to shine
He beats one man then two,
He makes it to the line
And crosses deep for you;

A dummy run
Has found you space –
Now one v one
You soar with grace.

His worried head just met
The ball he arrowed down
The ball is in the net
The keeper wears the frown.

The home crowd chant his name.
Once more he is adored.
Relief replaces shame.
'At last you've . . . . . . scored!'

Ian Blackman
Brighton and Hove Albion

21

Bird's-Eye View

**Come on City. Come on Rovers.
Up United. Up the Rangers.**

Like football? Oh no.
Love football?
Over the moon about football? Oh yes, yes yes.
Couldn't care a chirp who wins,
     who loses.
Couldn't tot a tweet about the skills.
'Offside'
The referee who needs bi-focals.
'Our ball'
The fouls, free-kicks, defensive walls, the clever
corners or near misses.
'Gooaall!'

   peck peck peck
    hop hop
    flap flap

I just enjoy chaotic crowds
(when they've gone home),
  because 80,000 people equals
    800,000 titbits
(when they've gone home).

peck peck peck
hop hop
flap flap

Terraces piled high with half-hot dogs in buttered buns, samples of sandwich, scraps of sausage roll, crisps and chips, and fruits of every flavour you could mention. Eat until we're sick, sick, sicker than a parrot (when they've gone home).

peck peck peck
hop hop
flap flap

Couldn't care a chirp who loses,
couldn't tot a tweet who wins,
but I wouldn't mind a replay.

peck peck peck
hop hop
flap flap

Up United. Up the Rangers.
Come on City. Come on Rovers.

Mike Johnson
Blackburn Rovers

Jambo

NO STUDS

Jambo playing football on the back field. His jeans rolled up to his knees covered in mud. Boots with no studs slipping and skidding. No-one watches except the tall cooling towers of the power station in the distance. No-one cheers him on.

CROWDS ON TERRACE

But as soon as Jambo scores, he's floating across the turf of Wembley Stadium. The stray dog yapping at his heels that jumps up to lick his face is the team captain's bristly embrace. And the women on the landings in the block of flats behind are the crowds on the terraces, waving banners that aren't really wet sheets after all. Even the hard-faced kids skiving off school round the back of the burnt-out garages look like they might want to line up for his autograph.

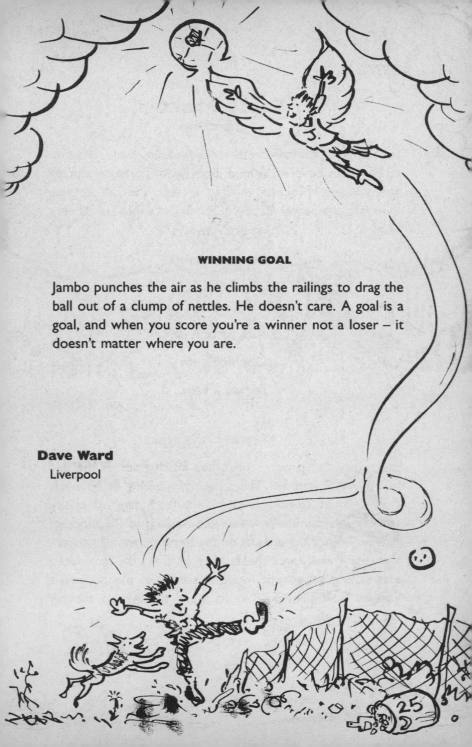

WINNING GOAL

Jambo punches the air as he climbs the railings to drag the ball out of a clump of nettles. He doesn't care. A goal is a goal, and when you score you're a winner not a loser – it doesn't matter where you are.

Dave Ward
Liverpool

Early Start

Where does he

get his skill from;

that body swerve

and fancy footwork?

He's a natural, sir.

Dribbled since

he was a baby.

John C. Desmond
Leeds United

26

A Passing Movement, with Nicknames

'Ghost' goalie bowls it to 'Badger'
who spreads it to 'Headbutter' Case.
He punts it high to 'The Fat Man'
who nods it to 'Old Fungus Face'.
'Face' holds it, flicks it to 'Skinhead'
(who's bald as an OAP coot),
his laser-beamed pass reaches 'Chalky'
who slips it to 'Six-Gunner' Shoot.
'Six' looks up, toes it to 'Loony'
who, foot on the ball, picks his nose
then he shimmies
and shakes
and nutmegs his man
and lobs it across to 'Red' Rose.
'Red' is a tricky big turnip
and he touches it off to 'King' Cole
who in turn traps the ball
on the penalty spot
and crashes it
into
the

Wes Magee
Swindon Town

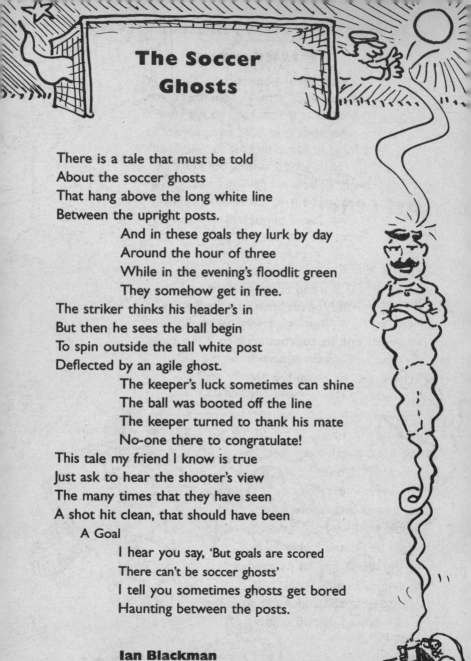

The Soccer Ghosts

There is a tale that must be told
About the soccer ghosts
That hang above the long white line
Between the upright posts.
> And in these goals they lurk by day
> Around the hour of three
> While in the evening's floodlit green
> They somehow get in free.
The striker thinks his header's in
But then he sees the ball begin
To spin outside the tall white post
Deflected by an agile ghost.
> The keeper's luck sometimes can shine
> The ball was booted off the line
> The keeper turned to thank his mate
> No-one there to congratulate!
This tale my friend I know is true
Just ask to hear the shooter's view
The many times that they have seen
A shot hit clean, that should have been
> A Goal
> > I hear you say, 'But goals are scored
> > There can't be soccer ghosts'
> > I tell you sometimes ghosts get bored
> > Haunting between the posts.

Ian Blackman
Brighton and Hove Albion

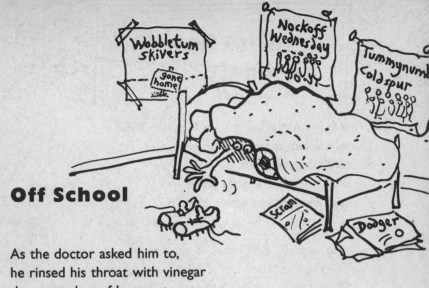

Off School

As the doctor asked him to,
he rinsed his throat with vinegar
then ate a bag of kumquats.
And soon the bugs had decomposed,
so he banged his bedroom door,
then hurried down the stairs.
Where was he escaping to?
Not school! Great Crikes, the thought!
He was heading for the park, of course,
with his scarf around his neck,
and underneath his jacket
a football. Would he play alone?
You bet! Unless you count the ducks
he curved those corners to,
or the sheep whose heads he found
when he floated freekicks in,
or the drunk he just persuaded
to sway around in goal.
And what more useful way to spend
a well-earned day off school?

Matthew Sweeney
West Ham

29

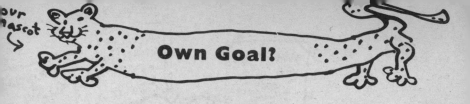

Own Goal?

We were due for a Cup Quarter Final
In the Junior League this weekend;
We'd trained hard, to make sure
That we'd get a large score –
But were dealt a grave blow by a friend.

Our captain, Ben Jones, is the reason
They've cancelled our Cupwinners' dream;
'Twas the worst of all shocks
When he caught chicken-pox
And then shared it all out with our team.

So we've penalty spots of our own now
And we certainly know what's the score,
For they won't let us play –
We're infectious they say –
And the upshot is we're feeling sore.

For a kick-off, we're out of the running –
They say we can't muster a team;
So, despite all our fuss,
They've disqualified us –
But, with luck, things aren't quite what they seem . . .

For (a week ago) Ben had a party . . .
He invited round all of his friends
Which included a few
Of the players he knew
From football teams other than Ben's.

And any day now, if we're lucky,
These players will show some fatigue
And start spreading their spots –
So what choice have they got
But to cancel the whole of the League!

Trevor Harvey
Arsenal

31

'L' Plates on my Football Shirt

When I play football for the football team at school
no-one takes me seriously, they think I'm just a fool.
My right boot's on my left foot, my left is on my right,
my socks are on my arms and my shorts are far too tight.

I have shin pads on my chin just in case I'm fouled.
My shirt is full of holes, inside out and upside down.
The laces on my boots are nearly five miles long.
I need two weeks before each match so I can put them on.

They told me to play sweeper so I borrowed my mum's
    Hoover
and swept up their forward's shorts with a brilliant
    manoeuvre.
They asked about my shooting and how I could attack
so I got out my rifle but they made me put it back.

I told them that my dribbling was the best they'd get
then dribbled down their shirts and made them soaking wet.
They asked me to play winger, I said I couldn't fly.
'Well mark your man instead' so I gave him two black eyes.

'Free kick!' said the Ref, so I did and watched him fall.
Nobody had told me that I had to kick the ball.
In view of this the Referee gave the other team the kick.
I was told to build a wall but I couldn't find a brick.

In the end there's only two positions I can play:
left back right back in the changing rooms all day.
I'm only a beginner and someone could get hurt
so I don't have a number but an 'L' plate on my shirt.

Paul Cookson
Everton

Are You Sure We Are Up The Right End

United! United! United! United! United! United!

United! United! United! United! United! United!

United! United! United! United! United! United!   'ello mum

United! United! United! United! United! United!

United! United! United!   city   city   United! United!

United! United! United! United! United! United!

United! United! United! United! United! United!

United! United! United! United! United! United!

Sponsored by Rustbucket Motors

Sponsored by ZAPPUM Insecurity Lights

John Coldwell
Gillingham

Eat Dog Food

Riddles

I've got a roof,
A wide front door,
A back door only for small insects,
A strong frame,
And plenty of windows for
people to see through.

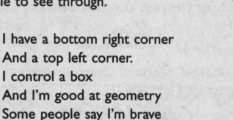

I have a bottom right corner
And a top left corner.
I control a box
And I'm good at geometry
Some people say I'm brave
Others say I'm crazy.
I can fly
And prefer my sheets to be clean
Who am I?

The chip spinning like a satellite
Arcs its way with computerised precision
To the striker's head;
To leave him only one decision –
To leave the keeper dead:
One orbit.

Scoring a goal

Goal-keeper

A goal net

Well, these riddles beat me!

He starts from the six yard box
Leaves ten astonished faces standing
Leaves eleven even more astonished faces
As he scores.

He takes his job very seriously
Never forgetting his keys.
Every evening after dark,
Come rain, wind or snow
He throws in a couple of old ones,
But on their birthdays,
He treats them to fresh, tasty new ones.

Ian Blackman
Brighton and Hove Albion

Own goal

Goal-keeper

My Team's Not Scoring

It's raining it's pouring
And my team's not scoring.
So boring no scoring
Their goalkeeper's yawning.
He could rest his head
In the back of the net
And still, we'd have no
Chance of scoring.

It's raining it's pouring
Now I'm the one that's yawning.
No scoring so boring
No chance of EVER scoring.
See me rest my head
On the shoulder of Ted
Who doesn't object
To my snoring.

Not raining nor pouring
Now the crowd are roaring.
Not boring not boring
As I feel myself soaring,
To deflect with my head
The centre from Ted
Now I'm the hero
For scoring.

Not raining nor pouring
I hear the fans applauding.
Not boring I'm scoring
Their faith I am . . . . what? eh? oh!
It's raining it's pouring
And I've just missed us
SCORING!

Ian Blackman
Brighton and Hove Albion

Detained at H.M.'s pleasure

No Football

The teachers took our ball.
We'd only sent it over the fence
for the seventh time that week!
But Kevin was cheeky to some old boy
who wouldn't give it back.
'That's that,' our headmaster said.
'We'll keep it now for a bit
          until you learn to play properly.'
Kevin tried to tell him that
we couldn't learn to play properly
if we weren't practising,
but he said it was cheek like that
had cost us our ball in the first place.

Kevin

After that there was nothing to do;
someone lost a shoe and we passed that about,
then made do with half a conker
and put up quite a dazzling display
till Kevin let it slip down a drain,
then took the cover off to get it back.
'You'll take that and yourself to the Head,'
our teacher said. 'And what do you think
        you were doing with your arm
        down that filthy thing?'

When Kevin came back he grinned and said
we'd lost our ball for good.
We moped around with nothing to kick
till later, behind the teacher's back,
we took it in turns to kick Kevin.

Brian Moses
Tottenham Hotspur

Goalie

I am the most popular player in the team.
I have just pulled off the most brilliant save.
I've got the ball.
My team are yelling and screaming
So.
I bounce it a couple of times,
Then give it an almighty kick
Right up the middle of the pitch.
Let them sort it out.

I am the loneliest player in the team.
There are twenty one players up the other end,
Leaving me down here.
I think we're in possession.
But I don't really care.
I prefer my own company.
It gives me time to think about things –
Like,
Can I touch the cross bar from a standing jump?

I am the most unpopular player in the team.
It wasn't my fault they scored.
I was hanging from the cross bar at the time.
Where was the defence?
That's what I'd like to know.
I can't cover for all their mistakes.

The captain said,
I can't be the goalkeeper
If I let another in.
Suits me.
I didn't want to be in goal anyway.
I'm more of an attacking player.
They need me out on the pitch.
So,
I won't bother to save the next shot.
Then I'll have just enough time
To score a hat trick.

John Coldwell
Gillingham

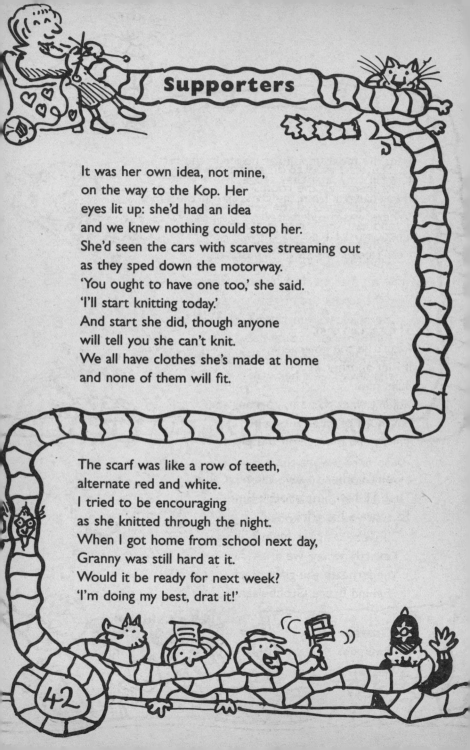

Supporters

It was her own idea, not mine,
on the way to the Kop. Her
eyes lit up: she'd had an idea
and we knew nothing could stop her.
She'd seen the cars with scarves streaming out
as they sped down the motorway.
'You ought to have one too,' she said.
'I'll start knitting today.'
And start she did, though anyone
will tell you she can't knit.
We all have clothes she's made at home
and none of them will fit.

The scarf was like a row of teeth,
alternate red and white.
I tried to be encouraging
as she knitted through the night.
When I got home from school next day,
Granny was still hard at it.
Would it be ready for next week?
'I'm doing my best, drat it!'

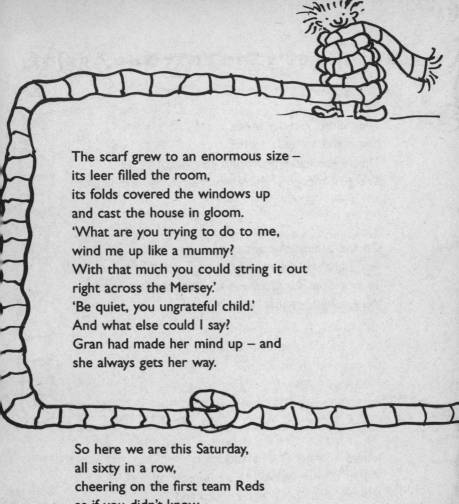

The scarf grew to an enormous size –
its leer filled the room,
its folds covered the windows up
and cast the house in gloom.
'What are you trying to do to me,
wind me up like a mummy?
With that much you could string it out
right across the Mersey.'
'Be quiet, you ungrateful child.'
And what else could I say?
Gran had made her mind up – and
she always gets her way.

So here we are this Saturday,
all sixty in a row,
cheering on the first team Reds
as if you didn't know.
If we're on telly, Mum'll know
exactly where we are –
underneath the giant scarf
behind Bruce Grobbelaar.

Jill Townsend
Liverpool

Wow! ! Let's See That One Again! !

They didn't exactly invite
Marie and Vanessa to join in,
They were hanging around just watching by
The goal mouth — there was Gary's parka one side,

On the other Weedy's bag —
And I imagine when they thought they'd seen enough
To work out for themselves which way the game
Was going they just, sort of,

Joined in. And all of a sudden
When Kipper heaved this pass to Paul,
Vanessa somehow intercepted and
Quickly passed the ball.

To Marie, who at once sent Rabbit
The wrong way, and after dumping Nick
Next she neatly side-stepped
Martin's size 13 Doc

Marten's, then bounced it round Yacko
With just one rebound off the Chemi Lab
Before backheeling to Vanessa who from all of twenty yards
Drove it past Kevin's despairing, diving grab.

Kev winds up with his head in Weedy's bag
And as five out of ten players plus Marie all
Jump excitedly about and punch the air,
He just gets up and trudges off to find the ball.

Then five out of ten players plus   Marie
Run towards the scorer to embrace   and fling
Themselves upon her. And freeze. Just   like the real thing,
Just like they end those replays on TV.

David Horner
Hull City and Warrington Town

(45)

Ref Rap

Clap clap
Clap clap clap
Clap clap clap clap
Clap clap

I don't win
I don't lose
I point the finger
Uphold the rules

I show the card
I send them off
I blow the whistle
When I've had enough

Clap clap
Clap clap clap
Clap clap clap clap
Clap clap

Fans all chant
Supporters sing
Can't hear the word
I like to think
it's

'We love
We all love
We all love the referee

He's brave
He's strong
His eyesight's great
He's not the man
We love to hate

46

He's the F.C. M.C.

He does
No wrong
He's always right
He's on the ball
He's dynamite
    And we love
    We all love
    We all love the referee'
        Clap clap
        Clap clap clap
        Clap clap clap clap
        Clap clap
    I don't get dirty
    Don't get hurt
    In my referee's shorts
    In my referee's shirt
It's plain to see
So you must agree
The man to be
Is the referee
    Ref ref
    Ref ref ref
    Ref ref ref ref
    Ref ref

Bernard Young
Manchester United

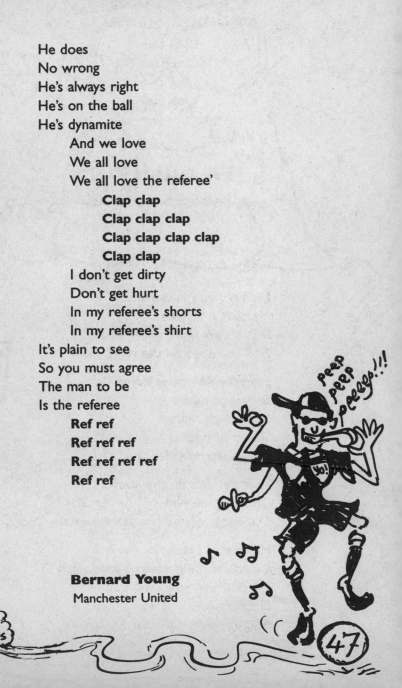

peep peep peeeep!!!

Yo!

I ♥ Rave Rovers

47

FA Rules OK

Life isn't easy in our house
My dad's a referee
He's always right, never wrong
And he knows all the rules.

Everyday he comes home
Shiny black shirt
Shiny black shorts
Shiny red face
Shiny silver whistle.

He races around the house
Checking the nets on the curtains
The height of the crossbars over the doors.

He doesn't like it
When the budgie talks back to him
He gets mad when the dog
Dribbles down his leg
And he booked the cat for spitting.

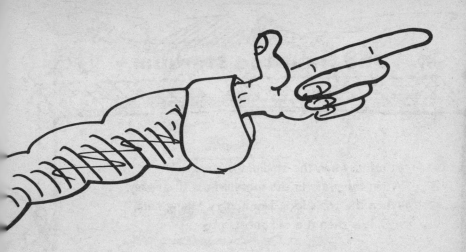

If we don't wash our hands before tea
That's it — a warning.
Leaving our greens — yellow card.
Giving them to the dog — red card.

Being sent off in your own house
Is no fun.
It's a long lonely walk upstairs
For that early bath
Early bed, no telly
And no extra time.

Yes, life isn't easy in our house
Dad's always right
And he knows all the rules.

tough lesson to learn, kid ...don't worry about it.

Paul Cookson and David Harmer
Everton and Sheffield United

49

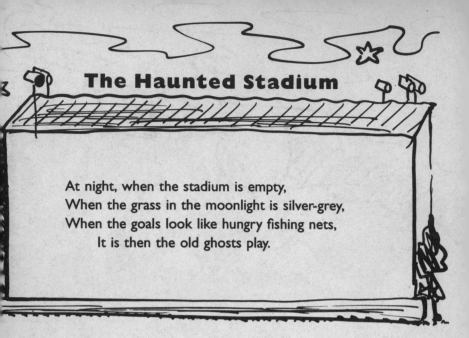

The Haunted Stadium

At night, when the stadium is empty,
When the grass in the moonlight is silver-grey,
When the goals look like hungry fishing nets,
    It is then the old ghosts play.

When all the crisp packets and fag-ends
And the drink cans have been swept up,
And the crowd has left, and the gates are locked,
    They play for the Phantom Cup.

Thin clouds drift across the face of the moon,
The grass stirs, a preeping whistle sounds,
And silent invisible spectators
    Throng the deserted stands.

And twenty-two ghosts in long-legged shorts
Dance the ball across the silvered grass,
A ball you can almost see, the old game –
    Run, dribble and pass.

Pale shades and shadows, heroes of bygone days,
Under the gaze of the moon, sidestep and swerve,
And crowds silently cheer as the ball floats
    Goalwards in an unseen curve.

Gerard Benson
    Arsenal

Worm's-Eye-View of the FA Cup Final

'That's funny,' said the worm
as it went under Wembley.
'I wonder why the ground's
so loud and trembly.'

Tony Mitton
Manchester United

Hope you've
enjoyed
burrowing
in this
book!

52

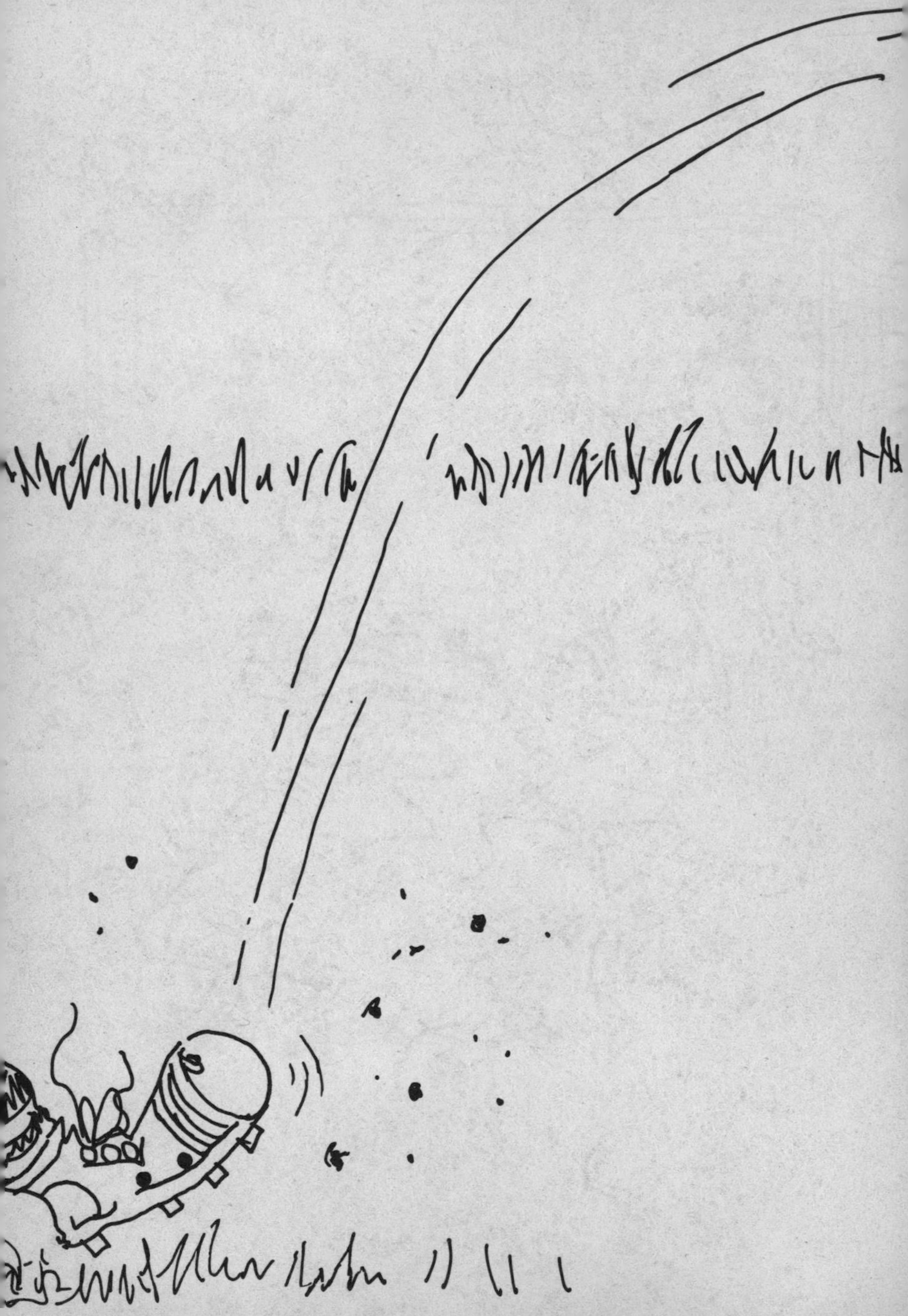

Football Facts

by Ian Blackman

Jargon . . .

Bench Place or seat where the manager, trainer and substitutes sit during game (also called the subs bench).

Box Penalty area.

Checking Moving one way, stopping to move off in another direction.

Chip A pass or attempt at goal made by a stabbing action of the kicking foot to achieve a sharp flight upwards of the ball.

Clean sheet A goalkeeper's ultimate aim of having no goals scored against (also named **Blank sheet**).

Close down To restrict the amount of space available to an opponent.

Cross To play the ball from a wide position, i.e. the wing, into a more central position.

Cushion Controlling the ball by withdrawing the surface contacted by the ball, e.g. pulling back the foot at exact moment of contact to soften the impact by taking the speed from the ball.

Deadball Any situation in which the game stops and is restarted by a free-kick, corner, goal-kick, penalty, etc.

Dribble With the ball, going past and beating one or more opponents.

Dummy Deceiving an opponent into thinking you will play the ball when instead you allow the ball to go past, hopefully, to a team-mate.

Football Facts

Early bath When a player is sent off the referee shows a **red card** (either for two separate incidents – two **yellow cards** = one red – or one major incident). This player takes no further part in the game, so may as well have a bath.

Engine room The midfield, the work-horses, a human dynamo. This position requires enormous amounts of stamina as the midfield must help out in defence as well as supporting the forwards.

Feint A deceptive movement with or without the ball.

Fifty-fifty ball when two players have an equal chance of winning the ball.

Flanks Area of pitch close to each touchline.

Goal-poacher A striker who posesses the natural instinct to 'steal' a chance to score. A top-class **striker** always needs the 'scent' for making something out of nothing.

Half-volley Contact with the ball the exact moment it touches the ground.

Hospital pass When a player's poor pass could cause a team-mate possible injury.

Hustle Putting an opponent under constant pressure.

Long throw A tactic whereby the throw-in is used like a corner, by throwing the ball into the penalty area.

Loose ball when neither side has control or possession of the ball.

Mark(ing) Taking up a position to tackle or deny an opponent possession of the ball.

Football Facts

Man to man marking Marking the same player throughout the match (becoming the player's second skin or shadow).

Nutmeg When the ball passes between the legs.

One-touch Passing the ball first time, i.e. without controlling it.

One-two A quick exchange of passes between two players.

Professional foul If there is a good scoring opportunity and the attacker is deliberately fouled. This **usually** warrants a red card without warning.

Red card The equivalent of two **yellow cards** really. A bookable offence. You're off!

Set-up (on a plate) Such an easy chance that even you or I could score with our eyes closed!

Striker Attacking player whose main job is to score lots of goals.

Sweeper A defender who is spare at the back and can read the game so any danger can be anticipated. Can also be an attacking player by bringing the ball out of defence.

Wall (building a) A defensive barrier formed by players to block a free-kick near goal. The goalkeeper dictates how many players are needed to make up the wall.

Whistle-happy referee An official who spoils the flow of the game by continually stopping the action for fussy reasons.

Yellow card First caution. In effect, a warning.

The Dream Team

Franz Beckenbauer BAYERN MUNICH and WEST GERMANY. On the 8 July 1990 he became the only man to have both captained and managed a World Cup winning nation (as a player he won a Winner's Medal in 1974). Formally a midfield player he switched to become a world-class sweeper and was his country's most effective attacking player. He acted very coolly under pressure.

George Best MANCHESTER UNITED and NORTHERN IRELAND. Won two League Championship medals and finally, in 1968, the European Cup. A tricky winger with a completely individual style. A great entertainer and brilliant dribbler with tremendous balance, which enabled him to go round or ride opponents' tackles or challenges as he twisted and turned his way to goal.

Bobby Charlton MANCHESTER UNITED and ENGLAND. The complete footballer possessing a marvellous pass, surging power and a cannonball shot. Won Winner's Medals in the FA Cup, League Championship, and European Cup. Capped 106 times for his country, scoring 49 goals, and helped England win the World Cup in 1966. A perfect ambassador for football.

Paul Gascoigne NEWCASTLE, SPURS, LAZIO and ENGLAND. A Geordie who left English football when he transferred to the Italian side Lazio for £5 million. His rise to stardom was due not to luck but to his eagerness to learn and practise his skills. Gazza's remarkable energy and willingness to succeed helped him shine during the 1990 World Cup Finals in Italy. Although no one player is bigger than the team, he is the type of player any manager would love to build a team around.

The Dream Team

Diego Maradona BARCELONA, NAPOLI and ARGENTINA. First played for his country at seventeen when he came on as a substitute. Helped Napoli win two Italian championships. At his peak he was said to be the world's best dribbler. Strong, with good balance, he had electrifying pace over the first five metres. He terrified defences by running directly at them. Banned from football in 1991 for a year after failing a dope test. Now playing in Spanish league for Sevilla.

Sir Stanley Matthews STOKE, BLACKPOOL and ENGLAND. League début in 1932 at seventeen and last league game at the age of fifty. Supremely fit and a perfect gentleman on and off the field. First footballer to be knighted whilst still playing. Neat and tricky winger whose skills brought crowds to their feet wherever he played. Finally won an FA Cup Winner's Medal at the age of thirty-eight with Blackpool. Won the last of his 54 England caps aged forty-two. The first European Footballer of the Year.

Bobby Moore WEST HAM UNITED and ENGLAND. A world-class defender whose coolness, vision and passing created many goals. England's youngest ever captain at twenty-four, he was capped 108 times for his country. In the sixties he captained West Ham to FA Cup and European Cup Winners Cup success. He also captained England to their only World Cup success, beating West Germany 4–2 in 1966. A true sportsman and gentleman, sadly he died of cancer in 1993 aged fifty-one.

Pele SANTOS and BRAZIL. While still a teenager (seventeen) he scored two goals in the 1958 World Cup Final triumph over Sweden. One of his goals is said, by many, to be the greatest goal ever scored in a World Cup Final; Pele took a high ball on his thigh, hooked it over his head, spinning round, he volleyed the ball into the Swedish net. Won the World Cup again with

Brazil in 1970. Regarded by many as the best ever footballer, he averaged almost a goal a game – during a career which spanned about 1200 games. A true entertainer with beautiful silky skills and the ability to create the unexpected.

Ferenc Puskas HONVED, REAL MADRID and HUNGARY. He possessed a thunderbolt left foot and had brilliant vision for a pass or a shot. In 1958 he signed for Real Madrid, receiving a £10,000 signing-on fee. Retired in 1966 and as manager took the Greek champions Panethinaikos to a European Cup Final.

Marco Van Basten AJAX, AC MILAN and HOLLAND. The best striker in the world today. Voted European Fooballer of the Year in 1992 for third time in his career. Father was a footballer, mother was a world-class athlete. Signed for Dutch club Ajax at sixteen. Scored 128 goals, averaging almost one a game. In the 1985–86 season he won the coveted golden Boot Award, scoring 37 goals in 26 league games. The following season he scored 31, and captained Ajax to a Cup Winners Cup victory. Transferred to Italian side AC Milan and was top scorer in the 1991–92 Italian league, winning the championship unbeaten. Also won the European Nations Cup with Holland.

Lev Yashin MOSCOW DYNAMO and RUSSIA. European Footballer of the Year 1963. Before making the first team he nearly gave up the game in favour of ice hockey. He was not only famous for his acrobatic displays in goals, but for his great sportsmanship. Whilst playing for The Rest of the World Team v England at Wembley, a scorching shot soared towards his goal – the only part of his body that moved was one arm as he jabbed out a fist to punch the ball away for a throw-in.

So You Want to be a Professional Footballer?

One You **must** have ability. This ability can be encouraged and developed by a parent, a relation, a friend, a teacher, or an organiser of an out-of-school club.

Two Football must be in your blood. To succeed you will need to eat, drink and sleep football. Dedication and the willingness to learn are vital.

Three Represent your school team.

Four Represent your district team.

Five Represent your county team.

Six Be invited to attend schoolboy trials at a full-time professional club. Be recommended to a club by your team manager or teacher.

Seven Be offered a schoolboy apprenticeship. Play for club's youth team, then progress to reserve team football.

Eight Be offered a full-time adult apprenticeship.

Nine First team début: your future at your feet, and in your head and heart.

Ten Alternatively you could be out playing semi-professional part-time football or Sunday football and, watching from the touchline, is a scout. He spots your talent and you are plucked from obscurity into the 'big time'. Keep dreaming, for dreams can come true.

A selected list of poetry books available from Macmillan

The prices shown below are correct at the time of going to press. However, Macmillan Publishers reserve the right to show new retail prices on covers which may differ from those previously advertised.

The Secret Lives of Teachers
Revealing rhymes, chosen by Brian Moses
0 330 34265 7
£3.50

You'll Never Walk Alone
More football poems, chosen by David Orme
0 330 33787 4
£2.99

We Was Robbed
Yet more football poems, chosen by David Orme
0 330 35005 6
£2.99

Nothing Tastes Quite Like a Gerbil
And other vile verses, chosen by David Orme
0 330 34632 6
£2.99

Custard Pie
Poems that are jokes, chosen by Pie Corbett
0 330 33992 3
£2.99

Parent-Free Zone
Poems about parents, chosen by Brian Moses
0 330 34554 0
£2.99

Tongue Twisters and Tonsil Twizzlers
Poems chosen by Paul Cookson
0 330 34941 4
£2.99

All Macmillan titles can be ordered at your local bookshop or are available by post from:

**Book Service by Post
PO Box 29, Douglas, Isle of Man IM99 1BQ**

Credit cards accepted. For details:
Telephone: 01624 675137
Fax: 01624 670923
E-mail: bookshop@enterprise.net

Free postage and packing in the UK.
Overseas customers: add £1 per book (paperback)
and £3 per book (hardback).